MW00342523

Tree Line

Judy Halebsky

New Issues Poetry & Prose

A Green Rose Book

New Issues Poetry & Prose
The College of Arts and Sciences
Western Michigan University
Kalamazoo, Michigan 49008

 The original publication of this book is made possible
by a grant from the National Endowment for the Arts.

Copyright © 2014 by Judy Halebsky. All rights reserved.
Printed in the United States of America.

First Edition, 2014.

ISBN: 978-1-936970-25-4 (paperbound)

Library of Congress Cataloging-in-Publication Data:
Halebsky, Judy.
Tree Line/Judy Halebsky
Library of Congress Control Number: 2013949846

Editor: William Olsen
Managing Editor: Kimberly Kolbe
Layout Editor: McKenzie Lynn Tozan
Assistant Editor: Traci Brimhall
Art Direction: Nicholas Kuder
Design: John-Mark Cuarto
Production: Paul Sizer
                        The Design Center, Frostic School of Art
                        College of Fine Arts
                        Western Michigan University
Printing: McNaughton & Gunn, Inc.

Tree Line

Judy Halebsky

New Issues

WESTERN MICHIGAN UNIVERSITY

Also by Judy Halebsky

Sky=Empty
Space/Gap/Interval/Distance (chapbook)

Contents

for pine, study pine, for bamboo, study bamboo
—Basho

Transmission

From the darkness and the fireflies, he calls me—
mapless, unguided, nightwalker

pulling night from clear blue day to that heavy blue
when there's still a little light in the sky
and the trees are dark against it

I am hiding in those trees
on a branch in the sway with the wind
not holding on so much as balancing

he calls me the night traveler
the angel breather
he calls me the one who has not come home

A thread for a nest, a word for a vein

She is sending cupcakes out the window
in a basket tied with string

Frida stacking flowers in her hair

Aunt Nina scrubbing blouses back to white

Emily sending poems out in letters
in the needle hem of a dress

she is trading pinecones for cookies
feathers for scones

彫　心　鏤　骨
carve　heart　set　bone:
carefully polishing a poem

it was later when all she could muster
was to sit at the top of the stairs
while her sister played piano below

it was after her nephew died
so many bottles into the sea

I have followed nights in moss
on the north side of trees

Li Po Loved Two Things

High as a skylark
I rest in the sky of this mountain pass
—Basho

Li Po loved two things: waterfalls and drinking

when the Emperor summoned him
he was drunk in a bar

Li Po wrote back:
    excuse me from your court today
    I am a drunken hermit

worn like these stones
water rushes past me
branches and trunks form dams
                those leaning-together houses
                   the fish stocks disappearing
    a tree standing still in the flooded creek

* * *

I left because there were whole towns without work
houses worth less than the water heater
fishing hamlets without roads
houses clustered around the docks
docks clustered around the fish houses
we were a generation that shipped out
there are a thousand songs about us
sung by those who stayed

the news says they've found growing numbers of cod
to me now, the stocks are still down
twenty years dropping, and twenty years when not one boat went out
it's not that they are fishing again
it's just that they might
and my laced-arm friends? my moose-land woods?
could we come back?
could they stitch us into the salt air
the wind-bent pines
a kitchen table
a mist-damp coat
the lingering blue dusk
are they counting us?

* * *

if this is the middle path
if I had to fight
if I were called to court
I'd fight with sticks
with ice-cold water, with direct sunlight
with reckless wind-spun seeds, the outer edge of a kite tail
the fairgrounds, the spinning teacups
if I had to pick two things to love

* * *

Basho looking down over the falls
in another country
hundreds of years later
picking flowers for Li Po

* * *

fish don't have ears
but they make love songs to find other fish

water is eight hundred times more dense than air

the body of a fish is as dense as water

fish don't hear sound waves, they absorb them

Learning to Dance

—*Kazuo Ohno Studio, April 2008*

The Italian had on silver high heels
her hair tied in seashells

while Sensei talked she whispered me the important parts

I am an old man carrying a dozen apples

I am walking through the train station struck by lightning

grass has light
milk has cream
these are things I need to remember:
        foil-wrap wings
        birds with fragile beaks
        the angle of the earth to the sun

these are the primary colors: plum, pine, bamboo
        liquor, denim, daybreak

the Italian
(plum blossoms finally in April)
she says,
   I was like, beautiful
putting in what was missing
the high heels, the apples
I was like to mean *the whole of me*

Tree Line

Judy Halebsky

Space, Gap, Interval, Distance

I have spent too many days counting
butter or cream cheese
4 or 6 or 8
how to piece in the hours like a layer cake

Lorca and your olive fields
Ginsberg and your mountain dream
I have been a paper doll
not thinking of the rain

間 *ma*
written as the sun
coming through the gate

as what we leave open
between us
so the spirits   when they come
will have a place to land

***

The day we drove from the coast back to Sacramento
the sun fell in broad strokes as we leaned into the curve
you were looking at me and I caught your eyes

wish I could have known it then
to mark that feeling in ink
as a stamp
a letter
something I could send in the mail
that would come out of the envelope
just as it had gone in—

carefully written
bled into
and only half parted with

A Breaking Word

There's that part
after Basho writes
old still pond
of pressing a fingerprint into wet clay

where the word *ya*
holds a space in the air
a cloud changes shape in the sky

make it a dash, a murmur
a breath on the inhale

this old pond
so many have tried to open

a sigh, a hum, a—

frog jumps in

sound of water says Hass
plop says Watts
kerplunk says Ginsberg

Walk the Line

Bend the spine of a thesaurus—
my shadow map, guide of distances
atlas of cities

if this book were a bridge I would trust my weight to it

late bloomer, mountain azalea, dwarf pine

the letters didn't always make words
there were years and years
when they just stayed letters

I have come to feel moss under water
I have come to put my feet in the creek

Basho and Sora on pilgrimage
write on their hats:
no home in heaven or earth
on this path we go two together

(monks on pilgrimage, *by two we go*
the monk alone but with the dharma
Basho alone but with Sora
me in the library with 20,000 other fools
and a mother who wants a postcard
a line on a Christmas note
a baby girl to walk
a two-wheel bicycle, a spelling bee
a pirouette, a finger to trace the letters across the page
the letters to make a song)

some say they fought
some say they parted in anger

after Sora stayed behind
Basho let the words *by two we go*
wash off his hat in the rain

at graduation, my mother, hands in the air
shouts, *it's a miracle, a miracle*

Snapshots

—after Adrienne Rich

gaijin
a person outside
an over the ocean person
a bar, a back corner, a without the right degrees person
a not enough person, a rough clothes, rough hands person
a carrier of feathers, a newspaper clipping person, a tin can
milk carton person, a straw person, a blankets and park benches
person, an unloved, a forgotten, a pretend not to see them
person, an earthquake, a tsunami, a person without papers
a person who left home, a person going toward home, a person
who has not yet arrived

* * *

Standing shoulder to shoulder on the train
we count the years between us

are you married she asks
and smiles this would-I, could-I,
shake-your-head, fifty-years-ago smile

save a square of cardboard under the tree for rain

       紅 葉
       fall leaves:
       small hands
       hands like fall leaves

I stitch a quarter into the hem of my skirt

close to shore
there's a place where the waves
are going in and out at the same time

       言   葉
       speaking leaves:
       a language

which means standing still

you're not married she asks again

to hold down in the wind
for an ice cream, a phone call

I stitch a quarter in the hem of my skirt

* * *

Koi fish see me and open their mouths
heart shaped, pink and pale
we grow as big as the space we are given

***

Out of the Gate

I have breathed into too many balloons

put my fingers in so many cakes

had my body scanned with fingerprints

written out my dreams in lines of the night

traced words into storm clouds

mixed water with mint and bourbon

made a bed from spidering vines

worn a wreath of grass cuttings, a raft of stickseed

there's a snail who thinks he's climbing Mount Fuji

the racetrack is filled with stars

All She Did Was _____ My Hand

—*Or* The Thermodynamics of Unfinished Love Poems
after Dean Rader

Between her milk skin and the way the air splits
between her pursed lips and a June blue dusk
she wants ground rules

count: beer settles to the temperature of air
count: energy can change forms
count: *you, milk skin, meet me on the roof*

1. between the two of us energy is neither created nor spent

unless of course gravity can take down bridges
dissemble kitchens
my other half at a bus stop in Nebraska
traveling east then north

note: add something in here about monogamy and what it does to us

2. I confuse inertia with entropy, but thank God for the internet
inertia—resistance to change
entropy—resistance to spiritual change
note: this statement has not been peer reviewed
or disambiguated

entropy—heat moves into colder spaces, we call this chaos
it's happening all the time

she wants ground rules
which involves talking
which is something I was hoping to avoid

I call her voice mail and ask: *who is Hegel?*

she says, *A = A*

Tree Line

Judy Halebsky

an affair needs this kind of mystery

we climb the metal ladder up
onto the flat roof of the gym
I put her cold hands under my shirt

count: 13 as lucky, 7 as something else

she says, *it takes energy to break the rules*

count: stop talking
count: milk skin, dumpling hips, attic room
count: the spaces

3. when her chilled hands touch me
it's not the cold coming into my body that I feel
it's the heat leaving

Garden Trees

Bent for elegance
shaped for wingspan
grown into the broadest spread of pine needles and leaves

stretching out the branches weakens them

ankle-tie heels, charcoal eyeliner, a strapless dress

to stay upright
we bend at the knees
dance with both feet on the floor
weight ourselves against gravity

it's not polite to walk where the neighbors hang their clothes

don't ask for a story you already know

grown into the broadest spread of pine needles and leaves

my sister says, *move to Vancouver*
so when Daddy can't see, you can hold his arm

Daddy says, *she went to the best schools, the best*

weakened to things that fall: rain, baby birds, piecrusts, spatulas,
feathers, bridges, volcanic ash, broken kites

prop up the branches to carry the weight
in case of lightning or electric love

in case one person looks away

we hide from things that fall

freezing rain, pine cones, confetti
the branches of other trees

Stopping between Whipped Cream and Butter

Abby at eleven is taller than me, rounder than me
has more freckles and knows everything

she can tell the difference between twenty and twenty-one
twenty-one-year-olds are cranky
she says and puckers up her face

pine trees live for hundreds of years
so they carry more scars

       a confession
       an orchid
       a hot air balloon

pine: to waste away through grief

birch: a tree with paper-thin bark

when I go home Warren says *you have a wicked bad
American accent*

there are all kinds of ways to fail

       a piecrust
       a snowflake

spring melt   June thaw
how to unbend   unscar

the birch tree
slightly wounded
is growing toward the sun

Along the Way

世に降るも更にそうぎの宿りかな
In this world, our life passes, temporary shelter
—Basho

To make his life bigger than the corners of a desk
bigger than 18 scoops of ice cream, a four-lane highway, a 747
he wants to get married

> *Christmas cake: to get old quickly*
> *evening wedding: in the nick of time*

a poet friend advises Basho to live within his means

> *spinning maid, sitting maid, window watcher*

first the house, then plates, chairs, butter knives, serving spoons

> our life, in this world, passing/falling, a temporary shelter

(the verb for getting old also means falling, the way rain falls)

> *a bride in the last flourish of her youth: evening wedding*
> *a girl, good until her 25th: Christmas cake*

> *pass over: to be left behind*
> *pass over: to escape*

our life falling the way rain falls

this world, a brief shelter

a newspaper hat in the rain

Halfway In

He turns under blankets to roll me into him
wakes to the sound of my voice

             a butterfly net
            a wicker basket
                 we sleep
           in the bow of a sailboat
    cast by storms
who loves who more   or less   or not at all

a tourist broke down in the 5th arrondissement
at the hospital they explained her psychosis
how she couldn't reconcile this Paris
with the city she thought she would find

a vase   a cloud   the stacked layers of air in a soufflé

so many things collapse   if handled   if pushed

when the wind comes up and fills the sails
we lean to keep from tipping over

to recover from Paris syndrome
one simply needs to leave Paris

but here   we lean into the wind

寝返り
negaeri

turning over while sleeping:
    betrayal

Watering

There are ways that I am watering
the same tree for hours

what if it comes out
we were never in love

the reach of the branches
marks the span of the roots

I water to the edge of the canopy

there are things that can't sustain being looked at directly

water does not travel sideways

the biggest risk is what we lose to the atmosphere

Rad.夕36

—Yuube *evening.*

Dr. Yu looks at me over the top of her glasses and concentrates

　　any port, any promise, any break in the canopy of leaves

Maya worries about Chinese medicine not being western medicine
I give her the words the doctors give me
pass them to her untouched

　　　夕　＋　夕　＝　多
　　evening + evening = many

　　多恨 takon
　　many heart roots = regret

silence fell on our house like a lid
not each in our own mouse corner
but me, marked off, as the one falling
the one who will be lost to the night

　　　streamline these words into veins
　　　this balance of water and air

there are no wings
no thousand black and yellow bumblebees
no microscopes, no x-ray vision
she makes me drink the forest floor

Dr. Yu looks at my tongue
feels my pulse in both wrists
writes characters in a running script
too much wind, too much heat

名残 nagori
naming the dead = a keepsake

a song, a vine, a break in the canopy of leaves

I have patients worse than this, she says

才子多病
talent child many illness:
whom gods love die young

別 *Betsu*

—branch off, diverge, scatter

Maiden, spinster, night lover
the one who lives alone

by alone, I mean leaving
I mean there are many ways to be blind
I mean ocean
I mean airplane
I mean fathom, glacier, marathon

months ago in late April sun
I learned the path to your studio
melting the edges of pine-shaded snow

pipe smoker, wine maker, waterer of moss
your beard scratching my shoulder
our shape in the window
half hidden by leaves

verdant is a word for this kind of green

there are bird sounds in the train station
so you can walk with your eyes closed

betsu: separate
used here as goodbye

the sun is burning your outline across the field
straw yellow to ash
I hold my hand up to the glare

betsu: to break, to scatter, to fly

Ink on Paper

If you want to remember me
trace my outline in the snow
slip me from the mold

resin from pine
sap from maple

if you want to remember me
stack jars of candied apples in the sun
write me a letter in water on the sidewalk

以心伝心 *i-shin-den-shin*
以 by means of 心 heart 伝 transmit 心 heart

china red, chrome red, vermillion
oil based, water based, ground from stone

if you want to remember me
eat cherry popsicles melting to your elbows

if you want to remember me
say these words in the dark:
barn owl, malt whiskey, stone angel

伝 *den*
transmit, convey, pass on

心 *kokoro*
heart
the inner thread of a poem

if you want to remember me
wash my picture in the pocket of your jeans

$$\frac{38}{39}$$

***

Dig Me up at the Riverbed

Dig me up at the riverbed
knead the air out of me
shake me down
reclaim me
from failed tea bowls
from would-have-been handles, saucers, spouts

I can take a thumbprint
I can hold the shape of your palm
the spines of a leaf, a chestnut, newspaper ash

porcelain is a certain kind of clay
luminous but fragile
weak to gravity, to other plates

mix me down with shale
with a sturdy field crystal
mix me
down
so I'll hold at the waist
so you can throw me thin
so the light will pass through

* * *

No one likes plates, he says
they take up too much space in the kiln

to fire porcelain, we'll mix it with paper
we'll pile in wood up to 1200 degrees

I can't believe how long we've been together, he says
as if we're at the beach in a patch of sun

a wedding band, an Allen key, a dress too tight

we need air and water constantly

closed with a brick
there's a tiny window into the kiln

don't look, he says
wear a glove to move the brick

no one likes plates, he says
they break too easily

I can't believe how long we've been together, I say
as if it's been raining for days

don't look, he says
hold your hand near it to feel the heat

* * *

Lay your snail spine as a mold for me
make your room into a leaf house
an umbrella in the rain house
bed of moss
palm cup
clay doorstep
telephone lines into vines
we, who are not yet kiln fired
we, who would vanish in the heat

***

A Left-Branching Language

In Japanese there's a grammatical structure for something
that just happened

fig trees have a second bloom, smaller and less sweet

        what forces work against gravity?
                what word for these kinds of trees?

Basho can write about a branch that swayed in the wind
        and mean the branch just now stopped swaying

        our nights shaded against valley heat, vining him into me
snails, aphids, bumblebees, sparrows

skin heals in tendrils, in scars, in lines, bumpy, purpled, not weakened
exactly but less able to fold, less eager to stare into the sun

           late August, leaves turning
      a sprinkler, a hose, we ripened, ochre dawn and were gone

Rad. 示 113

—Shimesu show. Nickname: Showing.

[Characters are arranged in dictionaries by 1) the number of lines
they have and where. (this is for students) and foreigners)
or 2) through radicals—the base of the character. sometimes there
is more than one and I have to guess who answers to whom and
who writes all the names down on a list]

示 *shimesu*: show, point out, signify, discipline, revelation

when I said, all the history we studied in high school in Nova
Scotia was the *Wars of the Roses*. she said, yes, well, British
history *is* world history

this [   ] is something I am trying to explain]]]

Water=One

—floating is about density

At dinner, he orders both beer and lemonade
I lean into him
away from whoever else I might have loved
to sleep in a cocoon of pine boughs
to run through the woods in the dark of night
to keep nothing in our pockets
we jump off the dock when we can't see the water
swim with the lightning bugs, kick through the weeds
find heat in the willows
make my body
of these things
an oar, a life jacket, a canoe

How to Crack Open a Beehive

One that has lost its queen

       when the frame is wide enough   even silence is a kind of answer

          purple pollen from lupine   gold from daffodils

              brownstones, trailer parks, a lamppost

the hive can't live like that

a sleeping boat, a park bench, a cardboard box, a doorway

                 which is closer, L.A. or outer space?

   we read humans into honey bees because they are diligent

     because they mate by dancing

because they stay together

               from Napa county, which is closer?

              outer space

         it's just that we never go there

Hojoki

From two suit cases and no boxes, I arrived
you picked mint in the yard
we threw our broken bowls and cups into the sea

hojoki: notes from a small hut, a basement room, a view of ferns

hojoki: a place to live after letting everything go

we signed in thistle
upstairs the landlord fixed classical guitars
he played into the night

there were stacks of grade six math problems
lists of adjectives and verbs
I sang in the bath until you learned the songs

hōjōki 方丈記: a ten measure diary

it's not that we were looking toward each other
we were sharing a bench
under a tin awning in the rain

Dear Dr. Mossman—

Your class began with waves and a yellow bus field trip to the ocean. It was September and already way too cold for me to get in. We threw a tennis ball into the water. There was a worksheet. We were supposed to use the ball to count the waves. This was impossible. How do we start counting? I wrote infinity.

Mom was just starting chemotherapy. I would get her movies and ice cream. I read the textbook at the kitchen table with its clean, distinct paragraphs that I could read over and over again.

I'm writing a poem today about water. Its four states of matter (which as you know aren't states but phases, because they change). We think of water as having three states—ice, water, and steam. But there's one more in the deep sea vents when the force of all the water compresses and makes something that's both water and steam. It's called supercritical water, which might work in my poem. It's about forgiveness. About the heart, as both flawed love and a muscle. So I think I'll be able to work in supercritical, where something we thought not possible happens in some place we'll never see.

I live on the other coast now with my boyfriend. He says the waves move through the water, that the water stays in place, that the energy is moving, not the water. I'm putting it together at a 16-year interval.

My mother survived because
she wouldn't listen
because statistics are just numbers
because the ocean is colder than zero.

I hope you got better students, who knew something about the ocean. I hope they won't find mistakes in these poems. The ocean, the Bay of Fundy, the tidal bore, the sky. I'm an unreliable source.

I'm using oceanography to try to understand
if I should get married. if I should listen. if I should swim
out with the tennis ball and count the waves.

Tending to Fall

To the doctor who tells me the levels are elevated

to Maya who says she doesn't have time to read

to the 5 am shift at the docks, the coffee shop, the bus station

   it's not about time

   all mammals need air

   those are just numbers on a page

to the orange tree outside that won't lose its leaves

to my mother who wishes I would come home

to this road built too close to the coast

   we need a bridge, a suspension, a brace
                              a trail of bread crumbs

peach trees lose their leaves in fall

   I am becoming the one who left

raised on misquotations, abbreviations, unsubstantiated claims

all poems are about love

the patterns in my blood: inconclusive

Rain on a Tuesday in June

The garden is bending
a little this way and that
with rain
moss green   air green   rain green

Stein in *The Making of Americans* writes:

Sometime there will be written the history of all of them

           Paris green   midnight green   viridian

        (she didn't know that there would be glowing letters and
backlit screens   that we could each write our own history
ourselves
incessantly

  one side arguing for truth   one for the impossibility of truth

this will cause snow to melt)

        Alaska   the Yukon   the Himalayas

        ((thirty-seven years old. San Francisco. 2011)
my mother and sister desperately hoping I will marry)
bending under rain
this garden)

The Ohno Studio

When he couldn't walk
he would sit
and dance
with his hands
dashing like birds

now at over a hundred
he is sleeping in the house next door

we take off our shoes and stretch

his son writes the characters:

雪 snow

花 flower

月 moon

some die like snow, he says
it's beautiful at dusk
and then the next day
where's the snow?

or a flower
blooming all in one season

or the moon
little by little
waning

* * *

After floating his hands in the air above his head
angling them out in jagged lines
balls of raw silk
a snail in a shell
he started to cry
not a little bit but tears streaking down his cheeks

window frames, roof tops, fences and fields, boney hips, knobby
knees, the dancing Antonia Mercé, I have torn off all the layers,
I have looked straight into the darkness, I have called spirits of the
dead, I have let them take my voice, take my body, I have brought
back what I have lost and danced here with them, my mother, my
sister, the years hungry and burned

one girl said, he's crying because he can't talk
another offered, he's crying because he can't dance

in this studio
I have laid down my fears
I have been easily hurt
snow melts, flowers bloom
there is getting up off the floor
the third pine
the ground, the sky, the space between
this is where I have danced
this is where I leave you from

***

New Year's Eve I Put Moss and Sand and Pebbles in a Round Glass Jar

—to Yuka, after March 11, 2011

Now I see how pictures work
how a painter plants a garden
how houses in the redwoods get no direct sunlight
how streets in Tokyo carve through friendships
how failures lean up one against another
how they put pressure on the fault lines
how earthquakes cause storms underwater that come to land
as waves
how water is not soft and shape-changing
how water can lift cars and take down buildings
how upstream is about which direction I am facing
how I am just strong enough
to paddle with the current
to wait for the echo when I call your name

Sitting beside Adrienne Rich at the Yehuda
Amichai Reading, Berkeley 1998

I remember the years without poems
silenced by marriage
that you swam back from

some wreck, some daughter-in-law
the poems dense and tightly sealed
at twenty-two, I could barely open them

* * *

On the way to the reading
Chana's talking about Amichai's next book
he won't let it out of his hands she says
it's as if he thinks it's his last

Amichai reading in Hebrew
Chana reading her translation

white underwear
hanging on a clothesline
under the blue Jerusalem sky

a man asks Chana,
but the blue and the white is the flag of Israel
where, where is that image?

she holds up her hands
widening the space of nothing but air
between her fingers and her palms
as if to say *this is how much we hold*

* * *

I sat beside you that night
hearing the same poems
breathing the same air
I introduced myself to you
as if to a stranger
as if we had never met

they say in a wreck we don't know which way to swim
they say to follow air bubbles to the surface

I was not cutting cake in a white dress
I was not kept in any house or any room
shoes, eyeliner, the hold of his hands
the hull of a sunken ship, the metal cask, the vining sea kelp
we breathe oxygen at any depth
we must come up in stages
so our bodies can reorient
all this takes time, years
the skin on my hands ages
anchor, seaweed, north wind

I list with the current

it was his last book

I only thought the woman beside me was Adrienne Rich

I shook her hand and she was flattered

she liked the idea

Tanabata

—from a haiku by Takako Hashimoto

七 seven
夕 night
や (ya)
髪 hair
ね
れ wet
し
ま still
ま (just like that)
に while
人 person
に
逢 meet
ふ

The night of July 7th
when once a year
two lovers as stars
can meet in the sky

* * *

while my hair is still wet

* * *

会う
遭う
逢う

to meet
　　a friend
　　an accident
　　a lover

会うは別れの始め
meeting is our first parting

* * *

on a summer night
with my hair still wet
we meet

The Distance between Romeo and Juliet

                              the distance between Romeo and Juliet
          the earth and the sun   the equinox and July
          San Francisco and Tokyo
          depends on where we are in the orbit   folds worn into denim
          phone calls   how we mark each other   how we count

          because it takes three days to fire a wood kiln

          because sand at that temperature turns to glass

          because the sun will last forever

                                        (not forever exactly
          but on our fingers, in wrinkles, in what we can count, a kind
          of forever   not sort-of   but a lineage, a genre, a kind

          because a steel buckle can throw off a compass

          because sand is worn away from rocks

                    because the sun is actually white

              but when we look at it from here

                              through the blue sky
                              it's yellow

Upright, Windswept, or Weeping

There's a type of bonsai called *Literati*
named after long-ago Chinese landscape painters
with angled trunks and branches
that struggle for space and light

in these tiny trees spectacular beauty and harsh conditions coexist
(this is a direct quotation from a man who thought he was writing
a book about trees)

livelihood—branches we twist to survive
means—(bread and butter) (sustenance) something we value
(in money or love) as in—he means the world

competition is a function of capital, the need to be constantly
expanding (from a man who thought he was not writing about trees)

we shape the branches with copper wire
they are at once fragile and elegant
        a girl at twelve
        a woman with shallow roots
        an ice bridge, a villanelle, a peeled bark letter
        an apology unspoken, held up
        branches that can carry the weight: juniper, larch, pine

On the Line

fact: he signed
fact: our boy, our cub scout, our Joshua has ten fingers, ten toes
fact: at twenty, he wants a car and a job as a firefighter
fact: they are not hiring
fact: our grandfather went from drinking fermented apple cider
through a straw in the barn to champagne on the coast of Italy
fact: for him it was that kind of war
fact: he said he didn't want to have killed a man
fact: there's so much room when the lines go across the page
like years they open up and then they vanish
fact: I don't need to tell you how they come back
fact: basic training is ten weeks long
fact: the sergeant transferred him from Florence to the south coast
overnight so he wouldn't be in town at dawn to fight a duel over a
boat ride with a girl
fact: he'll fight in cargo planes, in helicopters, in tanks
fact: he chose a pistol
fact: these mountains will be here and I'll be here in the mountains,
still
fact: he was a good shot
fact: he said it was luck
fact: unsign unsign unsign

Dark Matter, Pine Trees, Eternity, Room 205

Like a handmade ceramic bowl
uneven, oblong, dripped, bare in spots
Joshua departs for the army at dawn

birds fly south and return months later
by then they are different birds
it's not that they change
it's that the distance is longer than any one life

my job asks me to teach the history of the earth
with both science and the idea that there's a greater purpose
so students don't get depressed or have a crisis
when they learn
that our sun is a star that will burn out
that death is part of what defines an organism as alive

at boot camp they pound their teachings into him
how to fold sheets into squares
how to dream in black and white

birds know the routes to nesting places
they know how to cross the ocean

Joshua, be like water
change shapes
float
let sticks, discarded carburetors, broken glass
drift past you

first thing, they cut his hair
put him in uniform, take his picture

he looks like a soldier already, Eve says

Joshua, dug from the foothills
built by hand

a student comes to me with her palm out
holding a little green cone-shaped seed
from this, she says, *a redwood tree*
isn't that amazing

Basho on a Friend, Leaving

He writes *don't forget* as *remember me*

not as a voice, as all the misspellings, not as a   this broken skin

Motel 6

Basho left Edo walking
he slept at the side of the road

                                   a monk came to California
to give a talk and someone asked him, *where do you live?*
he said motel 6

               he meant, motel 6

                                 he said haiku isn't 5-7-5
it's two images that crash together
                     to make a third

trying not to keep layers between him and the wind
he slept at the side of the road

                         * * *

Basho wrote haiku at parties   to the host   to say thank you
to say goodbye   (my mom believes in education
as a kind of religion   (so I had to keep going to school
(even though I told her it's a big waste of my time)))
we had a Valentine's Day reading where the theme was bitterness
we read Margaret Atwood's poem, *you fit into me*   which is kind of
like a haiku   except it has a first person and a third person
which people say there isn't in haiku   *like a hook into an eye*
but that's kind of misleading   in Japanese the I-s and You-s are
implied   which is different from absent   *a fish hook   an open eye*

* * *

when the monk said motel 6
he meant motel 6
he meant under the branches of a tree
along the side of the road
he meant night is only so long
he meant start at zero
he meant now
he meant we rest where we can

Judy Halebsky

Rad. 网 122

—*Amigashira crown. Variant: net shaped like eye*

I ask Jacob how far the human eye can see
he wants to say forever
but he says, *you can see stars, right?*

I know then that he will never leave me

買   net over a clam shell: to buy

貝   clam shell for money

目   eye for eye

gambling is for when there aren't other options

how far I can see into the distance
depends on the light, not my eyes

Dear Icarus—

—*after* Failing and Flying *by Jack Gilbert*

I know things didn't turn out as you had planned
but for the record—I remember you   flying
into the bright July

it takes a wild optimism to get out of bed
to leave a message   to trust the direction of the wind

elsewhere, I am the bearer of a dead language
siblings I never knew come to find me
seeds from my great grandmother's apron take to the soil

we lie so close your heart beats through my ribs
we walk scarred
we love only with what we can bear to lose

Tree Line

Judy Halebsky

Rad. 气 84

—Kigame "vapor" enclosure. Nickname: steam.

気   *ki* : spirit, air, taste, touch, shade, trace

air divided = mood

taste color = to look hurt

feeling feeling = to always worry

to feel up = students influenced by communism

feeling already = spirits of the dead

My father is calling to me from both sides of the grave,
holding his thick dense body up by the railing, in the mist off
English Bay. he wants to bring me with him, to circulate his
blood, he wants to be someone else, younger, himself fifty years
ago, when it was clear that, yes, City College will strike, the
union is strong. he says bagel, he says yogurt, he says there's
three boats in the harbor and just one will carry him away.

Breath-hold Break Point

We sink, that's the thing
unless we've learned how to float

there's a page in the manual for how to rescue
two people, underwater, clinging to each other

Sister Carla calls the men at San Quentin *our brothers*

Phil lives by something called radical honesty

we lose track of which way to the surface

they say it's like being drunk
there's a euphoria, a kind of bliss

remember: air bubbles float upward

born in lupine, in Willamette Valley, in Oregon
this year's six Blue Fender butterflies

how many do we need
to count ourselves as having survived?

make these questions into a cloud
up in the canopy
this bark, a balm

under the low branches of pine
fluttering a bed of needles and resin

from here clouds form out of
vapor to water, a patch of cold air
they move across the sky
into warmer air, then disappear

Dark-eyed Junco (A Bird Call)

Redwoods grow up in shoots, from burls, from trees that have fallen

sing only in low tones
sort sea shells from tea cups

my father's planning his funeral
looking up how much it will cost

Maya says, good
I say, but he thinks he's going to die
she says, he *is* going to die

a collector of sand dollars, a writer of paper letters
my pile will not pile up

these shoots are second-growth trees
the old ones were taken down
when it was unimaginable that we would ever run out
when the forest was a vast, deep force
a place you could walk into
and not make it back

bird call, what say you?

keep singing

and that crazy lady will put out her seeds
keep singing and the clouds will break
keep singing so I can find you

daylight will show me your hiding places

they are not ponderosa, not jefferson pine, they are redwoods

but by then, you'll be gone

Bristlecone Pine

—with two haiku from Basho

Mission Blue butterflies lay their eggs in lupine
monarchs in milkweed

they migrate 2,400 miles
from the high mountains of Mexico to here
they travel in months and years
they live for six weeks

Mom says, *one lifetime isn't enough*

feed me a broth of chanterelles
make me forget with snowmelt and fireweed

butterflies can barely see
so they flutter toward any movement

> even a long day
> is not enough singing—
> for skylarks

remember: by the time they come back
it's five generations later

pupa, Latin for doll, between a caterpillar and a butterfly

remember: skylarks only sing while flying

remember: each tree has a name

bristlecone pine live for a thousand years
unless there is fire or disease or people near by

Judy Halebsky

sugar pine is named
for the sweet gum
that collects on its trunk
as a way to heal a wound

a butterfly sanctuary isn't for butterflies
it's for milkweed and lupine

over the field
clinging to nothing
a skylark sings

***

Notes

A number of these poems draw on well-known haiku. The translations of these haiku within the poems are my own.

"Li Po Loved Two Things" employs Basho's haiku:

> 雲雀より空にやすらふ峠哉
> Hibari yori sora ni yasurau toge kana
> Skylark/compared to/in the sky/resting /mountain pass

"A Breaking Word" draws on Basho's most famous haiku and translations of that haiku by Robert Hass, Alan Watts, Allen Ginsberg.

> 古池や蛙飛び込む水の音
> old pond/a frog jumps into/sound of water

"Walk the Line" draws on Basho's haiku:

> 今日よりや書き付け消さん笠の露
> from today the writing extinguished from my hat by dew

"Out of the Gate" alludes to Issa's haiku:

> かたつぶりそろそろ登れ富士の山
> a snail, little by little, climbing Mount Fuji

"Motel 6" alludes to Jane Hirshfield's poem, "Why Bodhidarma Went to Motel 6"

"Bristlecone Pine" employs two of Basho's haiku:

> 永き日もさえずり足らぬひばりかな
> Nagaki hi mo saezuri tara-nu hibari kana
> Long day even/sing enough not/skylark

> 原中やものにもつかず啼くひばり
> Haranaka ya mono ni mo tsuka-zu naku hibari
> Middle field/thing/even/cling to not/sing/skylark

The poems "Rad. 122," "Rad. 36," "Rad. 113" and "Rad. 84" draw on the layout and translations found in Andrew Nelson's *Japanese-English Character Dictionary* (Tokyo: Charles E. Tuttle Company, 1974).

The epigraph, *for pine, study pine, for bamboo, study bamboo* is one of Basho's teachings that was recorded by his student Dōhō. Commonly, it is interpreted as stressing unity with nature and discouraging subjective interpretations in haiku. However, I like to think of it as meaning: we become what we cultivate.

Acknowledgments

Thanks to the MacDowell Colony, the Millay Colony, the Virginia Center for Creative Arts, the Japanese Ministry of Culture, the Community of Writers at Squaw Valley, my dear Ensenada Avenue Poets, my friends at Poet's Choice, Marvin Bell, Joan Baranow, Alexa Weinstein, Yuka Tsukagoshi and the whole team at New Issues. Thanks also to the editors of the following journals who have generously published my work:

Blackbird: "Li Po Loved Two Things"
CALYX Journal: "Halfway In"
Clade Song: "Water=One" and "Dark-eyed Junco (A Bird Call)"
Eleven Eleven: "How to Crack Open a Beehive" and "New Year's Eve, I Put Moss and Sand and Pebbles in a Round Glass Jar"
Failbetter: "Dark Matter, Pine Trees, Eternity, Room 205"
Hotel America: "talent child many illness" and *"negaeri"*
The Journal: "A Left-Branching Language"
Joy+Ride: "Learning to Dance"
Mid-American Review: "Upright, Windswept or Weeping"
New South: "White Alders" and "The Distance between Romeo and Juliet"
Ping Pong: "Tanabata," "Transmission," and "A Breaking Word"
Poetry Flash: "Motel 6," "All She Did Was _____ My Hand," and "Sitting beside Adrienne Rich at the Yehuda Amichai Reading, Berkeley 1998"
Poetry Kanto: "Space, Gap, Interval, Distance," "A thread for a nest, a word for a vein," "Rad. 122," and "Rad. 84"
Smartish Pace: "Dear Dr. Mossman—"
Soundings East: "Breath-hold Break Point" and "Bristlecone Pine"
Sugar House Review: "Hojoki"
Runes: "Ink on Paper"
Sow's Ear: "Dig Me up at the Riverbed"
Zyzzyva: "Rain on Tuesday in June"

Poems from this collection are part of a chapbook that was chosen by Forrest Hamer as the winner of the Sixteen Rivers Press Poets-Under-Forty chapbook competition.

photo by Chase Clow

Judy Halebsky's first book, *Sky=Empty*, won the New Issues Prize and was a finalist for the California Book Award. Her chapbook, *Space/Gap/Interval/Distance*, won the Poets-Under-Forty award from Sixteen Rivers Press. Originally from Nova Scotia, she now lives in Oakland and teaches at Dominican University of California.

The Green Rose Prize